C YOUR WAY THROUGH—

C YOUR WAY THROUGH—

THE LESSONS I LEARNED FROM DADDY'S GIRL

DR. JAMES JONES JR.

&

JARAE' JONES

FOREWORD BY:
DR. ERIC. GYURICSKO, MD

authorHOUSE®

AuthorHouse™
1663 Liberty Drive
Bloomington, IN 47403
www.authorhouse.com
Phone: 1-800-839-8640

Published by AuthorHouse   05/16/2013

ISBN: 978-1-4817-3454-7 (sc)
ISBN: 978-1-4817-3455-4 (e)

Library of Congress Control Number: 2013905510

CONTENTS

SPECIAL THANKS

I just want to say a special thanks to my mom. Even though she didn't write a part in the book she was a big part of it. Not only is she my mom, but she's a friend. I can go to her for anything. Next, I want to say a special thanks to my father, because if it wasn't for him this book would never be possible. Also I want to say a special thanks to my doctor, Dr. Eric Gyurisko, because if it wasn't for him I wouldn't be as healthy as I am right now.

Now, I just want to say a special thanks to one of my favorite nurses/best friends ever, Mrs. Amy Clarke!! She was my nurse from the time that I was diagnosed with diabetes up until I graduated from elementary school on June 15th 2012. She was not just a great nurse, but a good friend. She could make me laugh no matter how sad I was. So for this Mrs. Clarke I would like to say, "Thanks a million!!"

Then, I would like to thank my teacher at the time of my diagnosis, Ms. Mary Beth Carreriro. It was not easy for me coming back to school from the hospital because I was uncertain of what comes next, but you helped to make the transition easier for me. So for this, I want say, "Thank you so much!!"

Lastly, I want to say a special thanks to all of my family for all of their support and prayers. I also want to thank everyone who helped get the book together because it's been a long stretch down the road to try and get this book finished. Finally but certainly not least, I would like to say a special thanks to God because if it wasn't for God healing me and allowing me to come out of the hospital, I would not have been able to have written this book and all my experiences wouldn't be the same.

DEDICATION

This book is dedicated to all the people who have experienced a crisis, challenge or circumstance in life that could have or should have destroyed you.

Have you ever felt hopeless?

Have you ever felt helpless?

Have you ever felt lust?

Have you ever felt frustrated?

Have you ever felt like giving up?

Have you ever felt like you didn't have any fight left?

Some storms in life you cannot go over or go around, some storms you just have to go through.

C your way through provides a spiritual and practical guide for making it through some of the toughest storms in life.

If you are reading this book then it's dedicated to you!

FOREWORD

Diabetes can be a cruel taskmaster. That "cruelty" can seem magnified hundred-fold when it is a child newly diagnosed with diabetes. In *C Your Way Through—Lessons I Learned from Daddy's Girl*, Jarae' Jones and her father, Dr. James Jones, Jr. share with us their journey from the scary days surrounding Jarae's diagnosis with Type 1 diabetes to their eventual embrace of the disease and the daily challenges it brings. Grounded in their deep Christian beliefs, Jarae' and her father provide unique perspectives on dealing with adversity that is applicable not just to someone with diabetes, but to anyone facing adversity.

I am Jarae's diabetes doctor. As a pediatric endocrinologist, I have the privilege of helping care for hundreds of children with diabetes. Part of that privilege involves caring not just for the child, but for the entire family. Every day I am reminded of both the joys of accomplishment and the struggles of inevitable setbacks that children with diabetes and their families experience. It is rare to have a family share that experience so publically. In *C Your Way*

Through—Lessons I Learned from Daddy's Girl, I am thankful that Jarae' and her father have so bravely put to paper what so many families privately experience. I am touched by the tremendous insight, positive attitude, and maturity beyond her years that Jarae' exhibits. Her learned perspective on her diabetes and its place in her life is refreshing to read for readers of any age.

Although the struggle Jarae' and her family face daily is called diabetes, this book is not just about a family's struggle with diabetes. Nor is it just for families who have children with diabetes. *C Your Way Through—Lessons I Learned from Daddy's Girl* provides faith—based guidance relevant to any family in crisis. Dr. Jones teaches us how to handle the inner **conflict** of "Why Me?". He builds on the idea of **commitment**. Not backing away from conflict, but facing it head-on in a committed fashion no matter what. Additional lessons on **compassion** and **courage** prepare those struggling with the tools to persevere and become a "true **champion**", just like Jarae'. Jarae' is a true champion in every sense of the word. WAY TO GO!!

Eric Gyuricsko, MD

Assistant Professor of Pediatrics at Eastern Virginia Medical School

Director, Division of Pediatric Endocrinology, Children's Specialty Group, PLLC

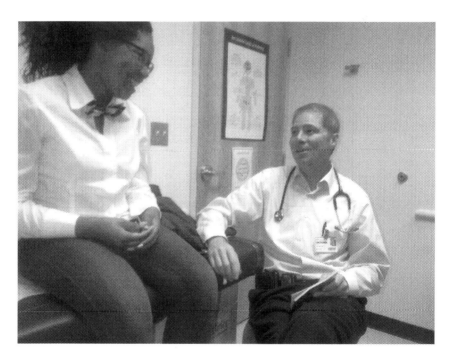

Jarae` & Dr. Eric Gyuricsko

A DAUGHTER'S PERSPECTIVE

Diabetes is a condition when the pancreas doesn't make enough insulin or your body stops responding to the insulin that is produced, so that glucose in the blood cannot be absorbed into the cells of the body. Some of the symptoms that I had were frequent urination, tiredness, excessive thirst, and hunger. There are two main types of diabetes, Type I and Type II. Type I is the more popular among children and is often called "Juvenile-onset Diabetes".

I have Type 1 Diabetes. I have had it for four years. You have to get needles when you start but when you get later into it, you can get this thing called a pump. When I first started, I was scared of needles but after a while, I got use to it. Every four months I have to get blood drawn so they can make sure my levels or blood are ok. People my age are supposed to check their sugar 4 or 5 times per day; you really need to check your sugar before you go to bed so that your levels are good when you wake up. If you don't, your sugar can be sky high when you wake up. If don't take care of yourself while you have diabetes, you can spend most of your time in the hospital, with your doctor, or in some type of place that can help you or try to help you get better.

When I first found out that I might have diabetes, my doctor told me and my parents that I had to go to the hospital. I was really scared. When I first got to the hospital, I had to have blood drawn so they could check to see if I really had it or not. When they got my tests results back and found that I did, they took me to a hospital room. I had roommates and sometimes I would be really loud at night. Other nights, they would be really loud because they check your sugar level and IV every so many hours. It seemed like every time we would get settled, it was time to get checked.

Most of the time my grandma would stay with me and my mom until my dad came back from church. I had lots of visitors while I was in the hospital like: Mary Jones-Turner (My grandma), Janelle Jones (My auntie), Javon Jones (My cousin), Veronica Robinson (Friend), Fran Clary (An auntie), Terrel Heckstall (Friend), Shack Heckstall (Friend), Jailyn Heckstall (Friend) and Joe Ratliff (Uncle).

When I went to the hospital I missed out on a lot of things. For instance, the night I went to the hospital I was supposed to dance at church so I was really sad because I didn't get to. Since it was during the school year, I missed schoolwork and tests. I was really scared at first but then something just told me, "Don't be scared, it's okay. You will be fine. Just do what they say."

When I first got to the hospital, my sugar level was 411 and they were trying to get it down so I could go home. I really wanted to go home because I missed church, school and my friends. While I was in the hospital, my parents and I had to learn a lot about living with diabetes and how our lives were going to change as a result of this new condition in my life. One of the things we had to learn was calculating the numbers of units I needed to give myself to correct my sugar level. For example, when I wake up in the morning if my sugar is 250 I subtract 135 (optimal sugar level) and I get 115. I then divide that by 35 and I get 3.27. So in order to correct my sugar and bring it down to an optimal level, I would give myself 3 units of insulin. However, if I am eating, I would count the number of carbs in the foods that I am eating. Let's say I am eating sandwich with 75 carbs. I would divide that 75 by 10 to get 7.5. So this would be 8 units of insulin. When I check my sugar prior to eating, I account for my current level and the food that I am about to eat. So using the previous example, if my sugar is 250 and I eat a sandwich with 75 carbs. I would add the two numbers together, 3.27 + 7.5 = 10.77. So I would give myself 11 units of insulin.

With Type I Diabetes, you have to check your sugar levels more often and give yourself insulin shots. After starting with the shot, I moved to what is called the Omni Pod. It is very easy and convenient. It does all the calculations for me to make sure my insulin levels remain normal. The first day that I tested out the pods was February 7th 2010. It was a big day. I had 3 choices of Pods to choose from. So for the weekend, I used the Omni Pod and I liked it very much so I asked for it. The programming process for the Omni Pod was not as easy as choosing it to regulate my diabetes. You have to be sure to program the Omni Pod right so that the time and the insulin amounts are set right so that I am given the right amounts on a regular basis and that took a while. When the Omni Pod arrived, it came in a bag with the pod, a Personal Diabetes Manager (PDM) for which you have to purchase batteries, a calculator, a log, a mini notebook and a food book call '*Calorie King*'. You have an option of a green or pink bag. I chose pink. You also get choice of green or purple for your calculator and I chose purple. Put the pod on by following these steps:

Step 1: Fill the "Pod" with insulin. The Pod automatically primes itself and performs safety checks to prepare for the delivery of insulin.

Step 2: On your PDM go to "More Actions" and select the option that you are going to remove the "Pod" from site (where you currently have your Pod on your body). Then select "Yes" to activate the pod.

Step 3: Put the "Pod" on the site and then select "Next" and then "Start". The cannula (needle) is automatically inserted and insulin delivery begins.

Step 4: Say "Yes" or "No" to let the PDM know if the cannula is inserted in your skin correctly. If it inserted properly, click "Yes" and then your PDM will go back to the regular screen or if you click "No" then you have to go back to Step 3.

When you are not diabetic, you can go as you please and eat what you want, but as a diabetic you have to count your carbohydrates. I keep track of my carbs in a binder but some people have books. Some people think that I can't eat or drink certain things because I am diabetic like regular soda or sugar gum but if you weren't in the hospital and did not get the education about living with this condition; then you don't know what I can or can't have. Sometimes people don't understand why I have the Pod and why it sticks through my shirt. When I get in the pool, they ask, "What's that thing on your stomach or your leg?" I just tell them it is medicine and I have to put it on. When people keep asking me about my diabetes or my Pod, sometimes it makes me a little annoyed or it makes me feel bad that I have diabetes.

I remember the day before I left the hospital when people came to visit me; I was walking, dancing and entertaining people. No one really believed I was sick because I acted like and most people treated me like, the same girl before we found out about the diabetes. The first time that I went to someone's house after finding out about my diabetes, it was Fran Clary's. I had a sleepover with Zykyah, my cousin. We had a lot of fun but of course when it came down to eating, everyone was worried out of their minds about what they could eat. So, I had to help them figure out how to read the carbs. It is really simple; you look at the serving size and then go down to regular carbs and you count those. Then you add those up. I had fun and my friend/cousin had a blast with me even though I had diabetes and had to take shots, she still cared for me and played with me the same way.

Right now, I have had diabetes for four years and I've been very good at what I do and maintaining my diabetes. I have had my insulin pump for two years and I like it. Every day I wake and before I go to sleep I pray not just for me but for everyone who has my condition and anyone who has something worse. This is what I say:

> Lord I pray that they can find a cure for everything that's out there or at least let the people have enough strength in their bodies to go to sleep and awaken in the morning. Let them also be able to wake and take their medicine. Also, let them be able to have the courage to be the same person and not have to be someone that they are not deep down inside because of their medical condition. Also, let everyone know that being afraid of being themselves is wrong and if people don't like them for who they are, then they need to let them go. And finally, Lord I ask that you help all families that are going through the same conditions or worse ones than mine.

> In Jesus' Name
>
> Amen

A FATHER'S PERSPECTIVE

On October 7, 2008 life seemed to be relatively good. I had no major problems outside of the normal brokenness that I wrestle with being who I am from day to day. It was a normal Tuesday night of worship. I was celebrating my 2nd Pastoral Anniversary, the energy and atmosphere was simply electric. My mentor and friend, Dr. Joe Ratliff acknowledged my family and as he got to my daughter, she began dancing with great jubilation in her seat. That night all she kept saying was she could not wait to Praise dance so that her Uncle Joe could see her! My daughter's name is Jarae' Emoni Jones at the time she was 7-years-old and she loved to praise dance for God! Her group, God's Little Angels, were scheduled to dance the next night.

"A Day I Will Never Forget"

The next day Jarae' had a doctor's appointment. Cheryl and I thought it would be good to get her checked out because she had been very thirsty lately and we noticed that she was having a little trouble holding her bladder. I thought to myself, it's no big deal just some form of a bladder infection. I was so confident that the procedure wouldn't take long. I assured my guest preacher that I would be able to pick him up for lunch that day. As we arrived at Rae's primary physician it did not take her long to make a decision that Rae needed to go to King's Daughter hospital immediately. She wanted to have her checked out for Juvenile Diabetes. As I drove over to the hospital fighting back the tears, I began to pray out loud that whatever it was, it was not something serious. Upon our arrival at CHKD, the hospital wasted no time going to work on Rae. As they secured her in the bed and they pulled out various needles, my heart dropped as I watched my little girl prepare for this unexpected ordeal. My heart had simply been broken into so many pieces!! At that very moment I put my sunglasses on to help hide my tears but behind the shades I was afraid, bewildered and stunned. This storm truly blindsided me. If you live long enough you will eventually have to deal with an unexpected crisis. These crises often show up uninvited and unannounced. A crisis can come at anytime and the only thing that we can control in the time of the crisis is how we will respond. It was confirmed that Jarae' E. Jones had Type 1 Diabetes.

4. I had survived the pain of fractured relationships and imperfect people.

I went through all of this with praise on my lips!!! I counted it all joy to suffer these experiences. "Yet this time, I had a problem with praising God!!!"

The conflict arose as a result of my daughter's medical challenge. As a pastor, I have encouraged so many others in their times of pain to keep the faith and praise God through it. However, in this most darkest hour, praise was the last thing on my mind. Several questions were racing through my mind as I sat there with my baby girl.

1. Why not me?
2. Is her sickness a result of something I had done?
3. Why her and why now?
4. How can I preach "Hope" when I am doubting God myself?

In moments of great conflict, testing and trials, these questions seem to occupy or consume our thoughts. The old saints use to always say, "Don't ever question God." At that very moment, I was not questioning the power or presence of God but the plan of God.

This was my 2ⁿᵈ Pastoral Anniversary. It was suppose to be a great time of celebration not a time of devastation.

Key Thought: God can mix celebration and devastation together to produce revelation. It is in moments of conflict that God shows us who He is and develops who we are. All of us will eventually have to deal <u>with a storm</u>, <u>a conflict</u>, or <u>a tragic situation</u>. When such occurs, we must seek to find God in it.

God is the Ultimate Developer. Like a good photographer, he does his best work in the darkness. Therefore, if you are walking through the darkness now, don't complain but celebrate because "God is developing you."

COMMITMENT

"Daddy tell them I have to get back to dance tonight."

Psalms 37:3-5 (NIV) ³ Trust in the LORD and do good; dwell in the land and enjoy safe pasture. ⁴ Take delight in the LORD, and he will give you the desires of your heart. ⁵ Commit your way to the LORD; trust in him and he will do this:

As one who has given himself to the study of leadership and religious scholarship, I thought I had a handle on commitment. Our world is filled with many people who can talk a good game. They have great plans, ideas, and schemes but very rarely do these people ever finish anything they start. I call these individuals "Spiritual Hustlers." People who are always seeking to make a bargain or cut a deal with God! Rarely do these individuals just commit to God because they love God. I see people week after week who put God on the bottom of their list of priorities.

Everything and everybody matters more than God. Many of us are easily distracted or sidetracked. It has become so easy for some of us to make excuses to God about why we can't do any better or our lives are simply in bad shape.

These are just some of the things that sidetrack our attention from God:

1. Pain
2. Bills
3. Lies
4. People
5. Parties
6. Money
7. Sports
8. Clothes
9. Work
10. Sickness

For so many of us any excuse is a good excuse when it comes to God!! However, as I watched the medical staff at CHKD hold my daughter down to give her the necessary shots needed in order to stabilize her condition, "The first and most important thing on her mind was getting back to church that night to Praise dance." This for me was the truest form of commitment I had ever seen. Her concern was not on how she was feeling but rather on what she had to do for God and for God's people through dancing. I must admit I was completely taken back by this because as her father, all I could think about was "God touch my daughter in order that she can handle whatever you are allowing to come her way." All I kept thinking was she is so young to have to deal with so much. Yet on her mind was "let me up and let me out of here!!!"

I could further understand if she did not want to stay at the hospital because:

1. She wanted to play basketball.
2. She wanted to play her Wii.
3. She was going to have a sleepover.

But not her—the one thing that mattered the most at that moment was not the "Pain and Pressure" but her PRAISE!!!!!

So as a result of watching her commitment, it reshaped my understanding of commitment.

What is commitment?

1. <u>It's finishing what you've started</u>. Life is tough for the best of us. However, commitment says, "I refuse to quit." Often times we quit just before our breakthrough simply because we didn't finish the job. Don't throw in the towel until God says it's over. There is still time on the clock and the game of life is not over yet.

    God declares to your today, that there are some things in your life that you have left undone.

    - Finish the diet
    - Finish the album
    - Finish your education
    - Finish your house
    - Finish the training
    - Finish the treatment
    - Finish the counseling
    - Finish the process to reaching your goals!!

If God started it then you should let Him FINISH IT!!!

2. Commitment is—not allowing your pain to hinder your pursuits. Often times we allow physical, spiritual, emotional, or financial pain to hinder us from reaching our goals and laying hold of our pursuits.

    Commitment is the seed that pushes us pass the pain we are enduring because we are so focused on the prize.

    Key Thought: Don't allow <u>PAIN</u> to rob you of the <u>PRIZE</u>. "Pursue it and you will possess it!"

3. Commitment is—remaining consistent even when your conditions change. In life change is inevitable. Seasons change, people change—but God remains the same. So often our focus shifts as our circumstance changes. One of the most pivotal things my daughter taught me that night was—even when life changes, our focus doesn't have to change.

- Stay focused

- Stay faithful

- Stay free

Commitment is realizing the "No" is not an option!! I saw all of these qualities in her eyes.

COMPASSION

Mark 12:29-31 (NIV): [29] *"The most important one,"*
answered Jesus, "is this: 'Hear, O Israel: The Lord our
God, the Lord is one. [a] [30] *Love the Lord your God*
with all your heart and with all your soul and with all
your mind and with all your strength.' [b] [31] *The second*
is this: 'Love your neighbor as yourself.' [c] There is no
commandment greater than these."

As the medical staff continued to work diligently to bring Rae's sugar down the next item of concern for her was her "Friends." With all of the pain her body was being subjected to and with this new level of uncertainty I was amazed that she had the mindset to be concerned about somebody other than herself.

For so many of us when we are going through our challenges, storms and trials, very rarely do we think about others. I learned something that day from listening to my daughter.

No matter what you are facing don't ever become so consumed in it that you lose concern for others. I believe she was physically weak from such a long day but spiritually, she was getting stronger. She knew that she was not just fighting for herself but all of her friends, classmates, dance partners, and teachers.

Key Thought: I learned that day when we put our pain on pause long enough to think about others, maybe we can also be freed from our own pain!!!

As I watched her in pain, I deepened my appreciation and my understanding of the ultimate sacrifice on the cross. While my daughter's challenge with diabetes is no comparison to Jesus' dying on the cross, it provided for me a tangible picture of selfless living. The fact that Jesus could pause long enough from dying to ask God to forgive us for His disgraceful death is selfless living. The fact that after all my daughter has been through she was thinking about others and not herself.

Thinking about others in times of pain and difficulty will free you from consuming all of your thoughts with what you are going through. We can experience deliverance from our situations when we learn to focus our energy on others.

COURAGE

Joshua 1:6 *"Be strong and courageous, because you will lead these people to inherit the land I swore to their forefathers to give them."*

Get Back Up!!

That night was one of the toughest nights ever for me to go to sleep. I tossed and turned the entire night trying to make sense of this life changing situation. The next day we had to attend this diabetes training class. I must admit being overwhelmed by stress and sorrow. I was not in a position at all to be able to retain the information on how to help my daughter live with diabetes. The staff was preparing us for how to live with it and I was still sitting there dazed trying to figure out how she got diabetes. Thank God I managed to survive sitting through the class without falling asleep even though my mind and body were totally exhausted from the pressure of it all. After the class was completed I felt like a freshman preparing for their first

Jarae E. Jones

Jarae Emoni Jones is the only child of Dr. James E. Jones, Jr. and Cheryl B. Jones. She is a very strong, encouraging, and wise young lady. Jarae is an inspiration to so many people young and old. Not only is she conquering her daily battle with diabetes, she is also conquering education as an honor student. She is active in several ministries in her church, Grace Fellowship Worship Center. She has the voice of an angel and she enjoys spending time with her family and friends. Jarae is also a Christian who gave her life to Christ at the age of 7.

For speaking engagements, please send request to Drjej2009@ gmail.com.

college exam. A lot of information to digest and not enough time to get ready for it!! I told Cheryl and Rae' I needed to step away for a few and handle a few things. However, the truth was I needed time alone with God in order to make sense of the situation.

"Knocked down but not knocked out"

As I approached Rae's room after lunch, I could hear a great deal of noise. I said to myself, it sounds like laughter but it can't be. To my surprise, yes, she was sitting up laughing and playing and had just finished eating.

What happened from the time I left the hospital until the time I returned a few hours later would change my outlook on life forever. After visits from doctors, nurses and other medical assistants, Rae's mindset completely shifted and I saw through her what courage really is.

1. She taught me that courage is not the "Absence" of pain but the ability to Accept our condition of existence and find the bright side even in dark situations.
2. She taught me that courage is not living in Denial but living with Determination.

3. She taught me that courage is not allowing adversity to Break You but allowing adversity to Develop You.

4. She taught me that courage is not born out of Comfort but out of Challenge and Crisis.

5. She taught me that Joy is not a Condition but a Choice.

For the next several hours as I watched her return to normal activities of eating, playing, and talking, her body language said "I've got this Dad." Her ability to fight this gave me the strength to face this.

Life Lesson:

Courage is when you have been dealt a hand you would like to throw in but you play it anyhow and you keep winning.

No matter what you're facing at this moment Courage can Change your Outlook as well as your Outcome.

Three Principles in order to move forward:

1. Can't stop

2. Don't stop

3. Won't stop

You've been afraid to take chances long enough; today—do something you've never done before, try something you've never tried before and watch God give you something you have never had before.

CHAMPION

Romans 8:28-38 [28] *And we know that in all things God works for the good of those who love him, [a] who[b] have been called according to his purpose.* [29] *For those God foreknew he also predestined to be conformed to the likeness of his Son, that he might be the firstborn among many brothers.* [30] *And those he predestined, he also called; those he called, he also justified; those he justified, he also glorified.* [31] *What, then, shall we say in response to this? If God is for us, who can be against us?* [32] *He who did not spare his own Son, but gave him up for us all—how will he not also, along with him, graciously give us all things?* [33] *Who will bring any charge against those whom God has chosen? It is God who justifies.* [34] *Who is he that condemns? Christ Jesus, who died—more than that, who was raised to life—is at the right hand of God and is also interceding for us.* [35] *Who shall separate us from the love of Christ? Shall trouble or hardship or persecution or famine or nakedness or danger or sword?* [36] *As it is written:*

"For your sake we face death all day long; we are considered as sheep to be slaughtered."[c]

[37] *No, in all these things we are more than conquerors through him who loved us.* [38] *For I am convinced that neither death nor life, neither angels nor demons, [d] neither the present nor the future, nor any powers,*

The final lesson that I learned from my daughter is what a True Champion lives like. Upon Rae's release from the hospital I knew life as we once knew it would not be the same. I wondered how having to take daily shots and the changing of her diet would change her attitude. As a father, I remembered struggling with giving her the shots she needed for her blood sugar!!! Then one day in the parking lot in the mall just before we went into the arcade I saw the greatness of a true champion. She looks at me and says, "Daddy you're not sticking me hard enough. I thought to myself just months ago she was tremendously afraid of the shots and now she is coaching her dad on administering the shots.

Life Lesson—You can overcome any fear in life by facing it through faith. She had grown to the point that she no longer saw the needle with "fear" but she saw it as her friend. That which she once struggled to endure, she now endured it as a good soldier. The reason this should be encouragement for you is because whatever you are forced to face in life, God can give you Faith to C Your Way Through.

Key Thought: You are not a coward but a CHAMPION!!

The next moment that I saw the true champion come out of her was when she asked if she could go over to one of our church members' houses. Cheryl and Jarae' are standing by my desk, one is asking, "Daddy can I please go?" The other is asking. "So do you think it would be alright if she goes?" I am sitting at my desk trying to keep what little composure I still had but, in the back of my mind I am thinking we just got used to giving her the shots and the blood sugars are being regulated pretty good—"Now This."

1. What happens if something goes wrong?
2. What happens if I can't get there in time?
3. What happens if somebody forgets to do something?

Then I saw my daughter grow about two feet tall as she spoke like a CHAMPION!!! She said "Dad don't worry about me, I will be alright and mommy is going to show Mrs. Fran how to give me my insulin." Now she has gone from the doctors having to do it to her mother and I having to do it, and now friends of the family can do it. Truly this was a sign of a champion. That she was not going to allow her condition to stop her from being the energetic, excited and enthusiastic young lady she was before all of this ever happened. She went that day and did not look back. Every other weekend she would find a friend's house to sleep over.

The last element of her living like a champion is she moved from the doctors giving her shots, to her parents giving her shots, to her friends of family giving her shots, to now giving herself shots and to living with and managing life with an insulin pump. She has taken what could have been a <u>problem</u> and turned it into her <u>power</u>. As she is giving herself the shots, you can see the spirit of a conqueror in this young life. She refused to allow her condition to beat her <u>down </u>rather she "beats" down <u>Depression</u>, <u>Anger</u>, and <u>Defeat</u> by always carrying a positive attitude.

Key Thought: If you want to live like a champion you must first believe you are a champ.

Here are three steps that I discovered watching Jarae' become a champion!!!

1. Think like a champion.
2. Speak like a champion
3. Look like a champion.

When you are going through difficult seasons or challenges in life learn how to encourage yourself. Each day find a reason to live and be great! True Champions do their best work under pressure.

Rae is a living example that "True Champions" might get knocked down but they get back up!!

A True champion does not always win every round they just keep fighting until they win. They don't <u>Give In</u> and they don't <u>Give Up!</u>

Be great today because God has created you to be a champion!!

SEE IT THROUGH

By Edgar Albert Guest

When you're up against a trouble,

meet it squarely, face to face;

lift your chin and set your shoulders,

plant your feet and take a brace.

When it's vain to try to dodge it,

do the best that you can do;

you may fail, but you may conquer,

See it through!

Black may be the clouds about you

and your future may seem grim,

but don't let your nerve desert you;

keep yourself in fighting trim.

If the worst is bound to happen,

spite of all that you can do,

running from it will not save you,

See it through!

Even hope may seem but futile,

when with troubles you're beset,

but remember you are facing

just what other men have met.

You may fail, but fall still fighting;

don't give up, whate'er you do;

eyes front, head high to the finish.

See it through!

ABOUT THE AUTHORS

Dr. James E. Jones, Jr.

Dr. James E. Jones, Jr. is a native of Chesapeake, VA with many educational achievements throughout his life. Dr. Jones is a man of many accomplishments. He is the Founder/Pastor of Grace Fellowship Worship Center in Virginia Beach, VA. He is the author two other books, "Broken but Blessed—How To Move From Brokeness To Wholeness" and "Meditate So You Can Elevate: How To Keep Going Up When Life Is Pulling You Down".

As a leader, Dr. Jones has inspired many people to live a life outside of the traditional facets of life in religion and everyday life as well as step out on faith when it seems that it would be insane to leave, step down, walk away, or do something that everyone else deems as insane. Dr. Jones through his own actions has shown people how to be courageous and humble under fire.

Jarae Emoni Jones
Age 10

Printed in the United States
By Bookmasters